Dog Hair

Isabella Gudiel

An Hachette UK Company
www.hachette.co.uk

First published in Great Britain in 2012 by
Spruce, a division of Octopus Publishing Group Ltd
Endeavour House
189 Shaftesbury Avenue
London
WC2H 8JY
www.octopusbooks.co.uk
www.octopusbooks.usa.com

Distributed in the US by
Hachette Book Group USA
237 Park Avenue
New York NY 10017 USA

Distributed in Canada by
Canadian Manda Group
165 Dufferin Street
Toronto, Ontario, Canada M6K 3H6

ISBN 978-1-84601-409-3

A CIP catalogue record for this book is available from the British Library

Printed and bound in China

1 3 5 7 9 10 8 6 4 2

Dog Hair

The best doggy hair-dos for fashion-conscious hounds!

spruce

Contents

Introduction 6

Short and Sweet 8

The Afro 10

The Bob 11

CELEBRITY STYLE: Doris Day 12

The Ginger 14

The Mohawk 15

The Beard 16

ACCESSORIES: The Cowboy Hat 17

CELEBRITY STYLE: Dorothy 18

The Pint-sized Gangsta 20

The Short 'n' Spiky 21

SIX STYLES FOR SHORT HAIR 22

The Beauty School Drop-out 24

The Pigtails 25

CELEBRITY STYLE: Meg Ryan 26

The Banker 28

The Skinhead 29

ACCESSORIES:
    The Elizabethan Ruff 30

The Punk 31

CELEBRITY STYLE: Russell Brand 32

DOG HAIR DISASTERS! 34

Mid-length Mutts 36

CELEBRITY STYLE: David Bowie 38

The Mullet 40

The Emo 41

CELEBRITY STYLE: Einstein 42

ACCESSORIES: The Gym Kit 44

The Soccer Mom 45

CELEBRITY STYLE: Tina Turner 46

The Perm 48

ACCESSORIES: Bunny Girl 49

CELEBRITY STYLE: Kurt Cobain 50

The Mutton Chops 52

The Nosy Neighbour 53

CELEBRITY STYLE: The Beatles 54

The Redneck 56

ACCESSORIES: The Bow 57

The Bunches 58

The Up-do 59

IDENTITY CRISIS: DOGS WHOSE
   LOOKS ARE SOMETHING ELSE 60

The Cleopatra 62

The Dye Job 63

CELEBRITY STYLE: Rod Stewart 64

DOG HAIR DISASTERS! 66

Long-haired Hounds 68

CELEBRITY STYLE: Cher 70

Le Chic Chien 72

ACCESSORIES: Beads 73

CELEBRITY STYLE:
   Jennifer Aniston 74

The Drama Queen 76

The Goth 77

CELEBRITY STYLE: Britney 78

The Dreadlock 80

The Raver 81

THE BODY ISSUE: ALL-OVER
   GLAMOUR 82

CELEBRITY STYLE:
   The Olsen Twins 84

The Farrah Flick 86

The Pocahontas 87

CELEBRITY STYLE:
   Amy Winehouse 88

The Beehive 90

The Rock Legend 91

CELEBRITY STYLE: Beyoncé 92

DOG HAIR DISASTERS! 94

Acknowledgements 96

Introduction

Welcome to the weird and wonderful world of dog hair, from suburban snips to Hollywood styles!

When man's best friend wants to dress to impress, he looks no further than the doggy hairdresser for inspiration. Just as with humans, a new haircut can create a whole new persona for a puppy, whether that's an image of carefully coiffed class, sporty sass or a blast from the past.

This book brings together over 50 of the most iconic looks. See the classic coifs we love (and hate) from the mullet to the mohawk, the bob to the beehive, as well as all-over looks like The Rock Legend, The Redneck and a little ghetto Gangsta. Plus, throughout the book, celebrity look-a-likes have been puppy-papped to show you how to create the hairstyles of the rich and famous in your very own home.

So, grab the setting lotion for your Setter, the curlers for your Collie and the dye for your Dachsund and get ready for a furry fashion show like no other.

Short and Sweet

The Afro

Not the kind of do that any old doggy can pull off, but if your pup's lucky enough to be blessed with soft, tight curls like a Bichon Frise, then you can tease them out and spray them up to create this heavenly halo. The aim of the game with any canine afro has got to be shape - it should be perfectly round and as springy as a Springer Spaniel. So make sure his hair is well trimmed beforehand and have a pair of scissors ready to snip off any straggly ends. Comb the coat out all over for a real fuzzy man's best friend.

The Bob

🐾 For fashion-conscious canines who are just too busy chasing balls and fetching frisbees to waste time getting pampered and preened, the bob is the answer. From its earliest incarnation as a practical cut for women working during the First World War, this sassy snip has been the mark of an independent woman. It keeps the hair from the eyes and is easy to brush out after a killer day at the kennels. Without curling combs or show spray, the short, sharp lines of this no-nonsense bob make any dog feel a million dollars, while also saving them an age in the salon.

CELEBRITY STYLE

Doris Day

A wholesome, outdoorsy kind of a gal, this perky pup is the all-singing, all-dancing classic canine entertainer and she's got a classic hairstyle to match. You might think that a triangle bob sounds like a recipe for disaster – more like an unsuccessful percussionist than a must-have hairdo – but she carried it off with such panache that women (and dogs) the world over now consider it a classic. Que sera, sera. Any long-haired pooch can be trimmed into this timeless shape, and the short fringe makes it a practical option for active puppies.

whippet-
crack-away!

The Ginger

It might have been a source of ridicule once upon a time, but today the ginger renaissance is upon us. Carrot-tops are cool, redheads are all the rage and even dogs want a piece of the action. Sadly, unless he's a lucky King Charles Spaniel, a very-now Chow Chow or a Red Setter, the odds of your dog hitching a ride on this particular trend are definitely not in his favour. Unless he can get hold of a ginger wig, of course. Working best with darker skin tones (for the more natural look), this is a sure ticket to hipster hound-dom, if you can get him to stop looking shifty in it. Just make sure you go for a natural tone from a reputable supplier, rather than the discount clown depot. He wouldn't want to be a laughing stock

The Mohawk

If your faithful hound would rather kick back in the sidecar of a Harley than hang out of your truck window, then this is the hair for him. Whether he's a baby 12 months or a ripe old 12 years, the mohawk is a surprisingly ageless style that shows this road dog was born to be wild. A mohawk can be tricky to maintain, but short- to medium-haired dogs with coarser fur will find this easier to manage – simply shave on either side of the central strip of fur and spike up with a tiny touch of gel. Add a studded collar and leash for a full-throttle look.

The Beard

A statement style for the pup who spends his days yapping on a smartphone, sporting non-prescription thick-rimmed specs and chasing neon fixie bikes around the streets of Williamsburg, the semi-post-ironic boho beard pitches just the right note between pseudo-intellectual bonhomie and rugged outdoorsman. A close crop on top highlights the bushy beard beneath, which gives him something to stroke during a 'paws for thought' over a flat white. Add a stripy sweater for a hint of French flair.

Some dogs just ain't built for big city livin' and highfalutin hairstyles. If your hound is more of a prairie dog at home on the range, then his simple soul needs only a simple accessory to match – the quintessential cowboy hat. From the 18th century, the Stetson has been the go-to headgear for every self-respecting cattle-rustler, bandit-nabber and sharp-shooting sheriff in the American West – and now it's the choice of canine cowboys too. Also good for hiding bad hair days from bitchy bandits.

Git along little doggie

ACCESSORIES: The Cowboy Hat

CELEBRITY STYLE

Dorothy

You don't need to see the Wizard to turn your dog into a Hollywood darling – just give her the Dog-othy Gale treatment. All you need are a couple of blue ribbons, then click her paws together three times and your very own mutt Munchkin will be transformed into the prettiest pooch on the Yellow Brick Road. Line her basket with gingham to let her really get into character. Use hair elastics under the ribbons if you want to be extra sure they won't slip out during a song and dance number.

Dorothy

There's no taste like bones!

The Pint-sized Gangsta

🐾 Does your status-hungry puppy want to roll with the big boys and make
his mark on the street? He'll have to do more than pee on lampposts. Fluff
out his hair and dress him in all the bling his little legs can carry. He'll be leader of
the pack in no time.

The Short 'n' Spiky

This choppy number is a close relative of the bob. Great for spunky pups from the wrong side of the tracks, this is basically a shaggy bob taken from a centre point, rather than a parting, then tousled and sprayed into shape. Highlights are an absolute necessity and go best with a splash of cheap jewellery and some leopard-print lycra. A remarkably durable do, this is one snappy style for one snappy dog.

Six Styles for Short Hair

Topknot

Similar to a ponytail, this sits high up on the crown of the head, letting the spiky ends shoot off in all directions. Not for the dog who wants to be taken seriously.

Natural

A girl's gotta have some down time.

Side Braid

For days when your dog's channelling 90s TV teens.

KODOG

KODOG

KODOG

Quiff

Scrape back the fringe and tie loosely at the back of the head. Back comb slightly and push forward to convert it into a quiff!

Bunches
Cute and compact, for when your pup's out and about.

Dare to Bare
Distract onlookers from a bad hair day by stripping your pooch from the neck down!

The Beauty School Drop-out

So what if your dog's getting on for seven? Show the world she's still got it! Tinting your dog's fur can make a bold statement, and this two-tone colouring will make her the talk of the trailer trashcan. Likewise, voluminous hair's all the rage and this back-combed semi-beehive is sure to help a little dog make a big entrance. But remember that, even if your pooch is eager to please and loves the limelight, she's still only small. Do all your curling, primping and styling in good time, so that she's not too worn out to show it off.

If your pooch dreams of long flowing locks but is stuck with short bristles instead, these pigtails are a simple cheat. Long-eared dogs can fake it using ear wraps, gently enclosing the ear flaps to hang down long and straight like braids. Leave a cute little bit at the end to finish off the look. A girly style that's perfect for injecting a bit of colour into a glum hound, but be careful not to wrap them too tight (or she'll really have something to howl about).

The Pigtails

Meg Ryan

This scruffy sweetie will win you over with a flick of her curly blonde cut and a wag of her adorable fluffy tail, but she hasn't always been so lucky in love. Under that tangled fringe she looks a bit fed up, and no wonder. Her tousled mane and sweetheart curls make her the ultimate pooch-next-door, so it takes the boys a while to realize that the utterly irresistible dog of their dreams was under their wet little noses all along.

I'll howl what she's howling.

Buy buy buy!
Sell sell sell!
Bark bark bark!

The Banker

Is your Rottweiler worried by recession? Your Doberman depressed? Your Pug poverty stricken? If the bottom's fallen out of your mongrel's market, then there's nothing like snappy dressing for getting him back on his four feet and giving him the scent of success. A starched white collar and tie (even if it's clip-on) will show the world that this dog is a go-getting business machine. And, of course, where would a high-flyer be without a print-out of figures that nobody understands? You can use it to line his litter box. Go get 'em, champ.

The Skinhead

Hair doesn't come much shorter than this. The go-to get-up for a hound who knows what he likes and would defend it to the death, closely cropped, coarse hair can make a pup look pretty tough, but doesn't mean he's a bad dog. He might look most at home wearing a thick studded collar with workboots in his mouth, but he's really got a heart of gold. A healthy diet and regular baths should keep the coat in gleaming condition and stop him looking too rough and ready.

ACCESSORIES: The Elizabethan Ruff

🐾 *'I have the body of a weak and feeble puppy, but I have the heart and stomach (and enormous ruff) of a queen!'* So may sayeth any right royal dog who can lay claim to this most elegant of Elizabethan accessories. Some puppies can't boast the bouffant hair that their chubbier canine chums can, so they need a little help from history to make a big impression. The ruff was originally designed as a practical collar, but soon became more of a status symbol, sometimes up to 30 cm (1 foot) wide. All the dogs on the block will be bowing and scraping as your dandy dog promenades past. Plus it doubles up as a handy cone collar for when she's feeling royally unwell.

Never mind the dog's b*$%!cks

The Punk

🐾 The style of choice for the puppy with attitude who loves to growl and howl along with the Sex Pistols. So what if he's a puny pooch whose little legs make a walk round the block a marathon effort? Who cares if he's vertically- challenged and mostly hairless? No matter how diminutive your dog might be, a bit of poochy punk shows that this mutt's not to be messed with. Mohicans can be styled and set with natural ingredients like sugar and water, rather than hairspray. Add a studded collar for a night out and he can really channel his inner Johnny Rottenweiler.

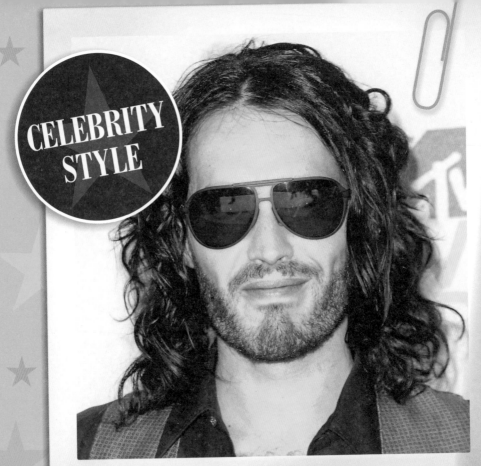

Russell Brand

This bit of ruff is a real hit with the ladies. The girls just can't help running their hands through his messy, matted curls, so his back-combed locks seem to stick out in all directions. It'll be tough to tame this hound, but keep his hair under control with a few well-placed accessories – some oversized shades will keep the fringe out of his face and help him to blend right in on the Sunset Strip.

Dog Hair DISASTERS!

Little pups who try to big themselves up with bouffant hair can end up looking like back-seat nodding dogs.

Beards look great if you can grow them, but adolescent wisps can be really disappointing.

This puppy's bunches were pulled too tight, driving her cross-eyed.

When good bobs turn bad. Bed head is a good look for some, but this dog looks like she's been hit by a bombshell.

KODOG

KODOG

All men of a certain age suffer from ear hair, but that's no reason to let it get out of control!

Make sure your dog can handle the hairdryer setting before you start styling.

Mid-length Mutts

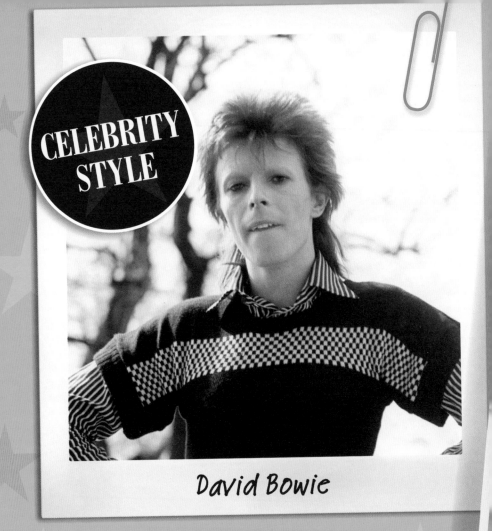

David Bowie

With a shock of shaggy red hair that's out of this world, there's no greater hair icon for those dogs blessed with the right kind of fur than David Bow-Wowie. This Pomeranian puppy's fluffy fur and teddy-bear ears may make him look more like his alien alter-ago, Ziggy Starpup, but they also give him an individual, intergalactic glamour. This little dog loves to dress up, but don't try to recreate that signature strip of lightning on his face.

The Mullet

Doggy business at the front, pooch party at the back and one of the most enduring dog hairstyles – you don't get a more classic 80s canine cut than the mutt mullet. Many owners worry about their pup's ability to see out from under a mop of shaggy hair, but want to keep the length everywhere else. This is the best of both worlds and a practical choice for pooches – or their owners – with a penchant for ice-hockey, Hulk Hogan or the early *Lethal Weapon* movies.

The Emo

Nobody understands how he feels! Maybe a fledgling goatee and a sharp fringe would help your tortured hound express himself. If your pup's going through the terrible twos (the doggy equivalent of those troublesome teens), then this hairstyle is the expression of angst he's been waiting for. A deadly straight fringe falling over one eye is the ultimate emo style and gives him something to peer out of when taking high-contrast pictures for his MySpace profile.

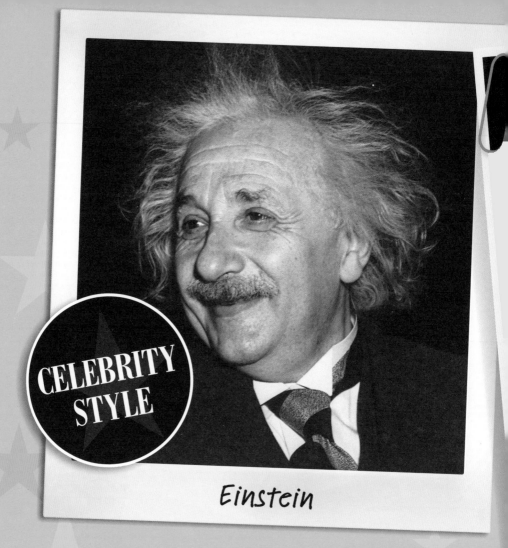

Einstein

One bright spark, this canine Einstein can calculate the trajectory of a tennis ball to the nearest millimetre and travels faster than the speed of light at the sound of dog food hitting the dinner bowl. Those wisps of white hair stick out in great tufts to show just how much is going on in that hairy head of his. Brush them out at the sides while flattening the top for a style that's out of this world.

What dog wouldn't chase a rabbit? How about a gym bunny? Opt for a workout rather than walkies and get the right look for all that lift and stretch. Comb your pup's hair neatly and keep it off her face with a flannel sweatband. The essential legwarmers are easy to rustle up on a home sewing machine or are available in all good 80s sports outlets.

ACCESSORIES: The Gym Kit

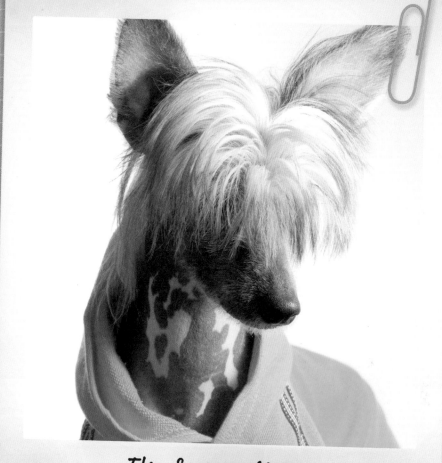

The Soccer Mom

She's spawned a litter a year and each one's a winner. Fiercely proud of her pack, this is one parent who'll have your hand off if you get on the wrong side of her or her puppies. With a personality as spiky as her hairstyle, whether she's scampering after a stray pup or yapping at a passing Rottweiler who's rubbed her up the wrong way, this petite pooch packs a big punch. But she's not just living for the kids. With a choppy peroxide blonde bob and an all-over body wax, she's out to prove that she's not over the hill yet.

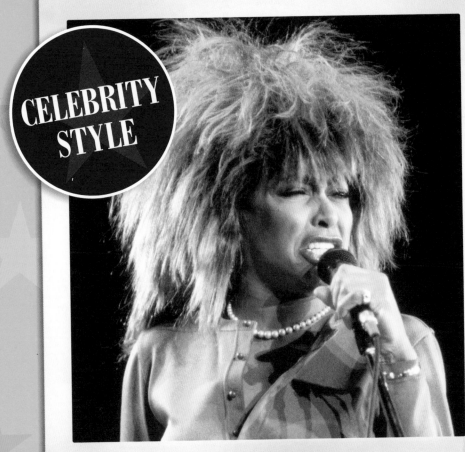

Tina Turner

Thicker than thatch and larger than life, the Queen of Rock's bouffant hair makes a real statement as a doggie do. A beast of a lion's mane, it's wilder than a night out in the Thunderdome. It's a simple back comb of the hair around the head, making sure it stays choppy. Long-haired breeds won't have a problem with upkeep, but shorter breeds might well be heard to shout, 'What've Pugs Got To Do With It?'. Remember to brush it through once the night is done to avoid nasty tangles in the morning.

The Perm

You couldn't move in the 80s for perming lotion and crimping irons. From soccer stars to TV celebrities, hair was big, it was back combed and it was curly. If you want to relive those glory days of rock and roll ringlets, but can't face the public ridicule, what better way than to style your dog instead? From fair-haired to brunette breeds, many have tight curls that can instantly be cropped into the distinctive shaggy strands you remember so well. But if your dog's fur is not quite so tightly wound, don't be tempted to add any type of perming lotion to persuade it. Like Michael Bolton's perm, some things weren't meant to be.

Does your dog demand to be pampered despite being a breed that's more suited to sheep-farming than show business? Does she hound you for attention? Sounds like your pup has delusions of being a doggy diva. What better gift to give the dog that fancies herself as Hugh Hefner's next big thing than the quintessential sign of a luscious lady of leisure – the Playboy Bunny ears? Who cares if she looks ridiculous? She'll lap up the attention like an X *Factor* auditionee.

ACCESSORIES: Bunny Girl

CELEBRITY STYLE

Kurt Cobain

This shaggy sniffer dog is pretty spaced out and takes a fairly Come As You Are attitude to presentation. But his scruffy style makes grunge look good. Lanky locks form a curtain around the face and you can just about hear his gravelly growl from under that thick fringe. A sensitive soul with a spiritual side, he's unlikely to find Nirvana without a bit of a trim now and then.

The Mutton Chops

![paw] This style is perfect for the dog who remains straight-backed and motionless for hours of the day. Like a fine oil portrait, only his eyes move to follow you around the room, all the while wearing an expression faintly suggestive of both exasperation and disdain. The handsome hound's mutton chops can be brushed out to encourage more voluptuous curls and then closely arranged around the face. Place a gilt frame around his favourite sitting spot for maximum effect.

I'm not one to bitch, but...

The Nosy Neighbour

🐾 In and out of every backyard, peering out the window whenever anyone walks past, sniffing round fences and digging through the flowerbeds, this old maid is one prying puppy. Snoopier than Snoopy, her wet little nose is in everyone's business and she's the first to know when there's a new face on the block or mischief being made. Of course, no self-respecting gossip merchant would be seen out without her hair properly set and her headscarf in place.

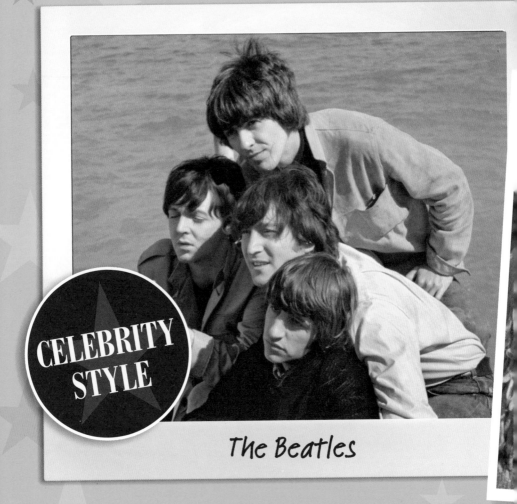

The Beatles

It's been a Hard Day's Night, and they've been working like a dog, so these laid-back, lovable, mop-topped mutts want nothing more than for you to take them for a walk down Penny Lane or play fetch through Strawberry Fields Forever. Just don't forget to pick up their Love, Love Me Doo-doo. Plenty of breeds suit a bowl cut, but do make sure they can still see through their furry fringe.

The Redneck

If your dog's idea of a good time is eating road-kill squirrel, then you've found the perfect hairstyle for him. The redneck looks best on hounds with a hangdog expression, bloodshot eyes and a dappling of liver spots from all the late nights howling at his family and drinking cheap whiskey. Basically a mullet, but where you'd have business at the front, now you have a buzzed mohawk that takes him straight back to the Doggie Prom '92.

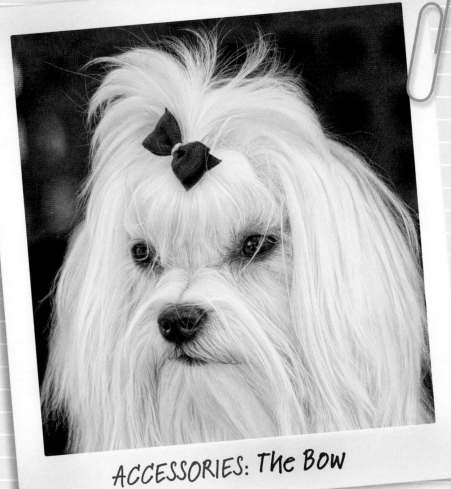

ACCESSORIES: The Bow

When your pooch starts getting picky, bad-tempered or downright bitchy, then knick-knack, patty-whack, give your dog a bow! The simplest of hairstyling accessories, this versatile ornament instantly gives a bit of girlish charm to a grumpy puppy. Great for topping off a topknot, bows can also be added to a puppy's ponytail, actual tail or just clipped anywhere on her coat at a jaunty angle. Equally suited to short- or long-haired dogs, bows might not make your dog any better behaved, but she'll definitely look cuter as she chews up your slippers and shreds your mail.

The Bunches

When your Bichon Frise is frizzy, your Poodle's too poofy, or your Terrier's too tatty, look no further than basic bunches to banish any bad hair day. It only takes two hair elastics and instantly lifts a shaggy mane into a manageable style. You can brush the bunches out for extra impact, convincing everyone that the frizzy fur was always intentional. So easy anyone could do it, the hardest thing about this hairstyle is getting your frisky friend to keep still!

A picture in peroxide blonde! A vision with volume. The classic up-do is perfect for the dog who wants to distract from her patchy skin or balding coat and still feel like a beauty queen. Trim the hair so that it falls in feathered layers to just below the jaw line, thinning it out around the face so she can still see! This works best on breeds whose ears stand up, but back combing the roots of her hair will help to boost it. Allow the hair further back to fall onto her shoulders, and she'll look like a princess ready to meet her Pup Charming.

The Up-do

IDENTITY CRISIS: Dogs Whose Looks are Something Else

Bear Just as grumpy when you wake him up, but better behaved at a picnic.

Mop Only running him around the floor doesn't make it any cleaner.

Beatnik This hound dog digs Alan Ginsberg's 'Howl'.

KODOG

KODOG

Chinese Dragon Bring luck and good fortune into your life as he weaves his way around your home.

Pirate Avast, ye scurvy sea dog!

Sporran What a Scotsman keeps over his kilt.

61

The Cleopatra

The original diva and a powerful presence in Ancient Egypt, Cleopatra was also a queen of the coiffures. Her blunt-cropped long bob is an iconic style even today, and your dog will cut a fine, Pharaoh-ish figure following in her footsteps. Dark hair means that the traditional heavy kohl eyeliner is probably unnecessary, but adorn with a gold headdress for a real regal look. Draw the line at letting her bathe in milk, though, unless you want her style to turn sour.

The Dye Job

Show off a puppy who's larger and louder than life to the world (or warn it she's coming) with a bright doggie dye that will really set her apart from the canine crowd. Non-toxic dog hair colourants – from neon pink to garish green, the sky's the limit – are available from pet-grooming stores, but do remember that human dye is a big no-no and to do a skin text first unless you want your mutt to moult. Whether she's throwing shapes at a party or chasing sticks in the park, a streak of shocking bubblegum pink is sure to turn heads.

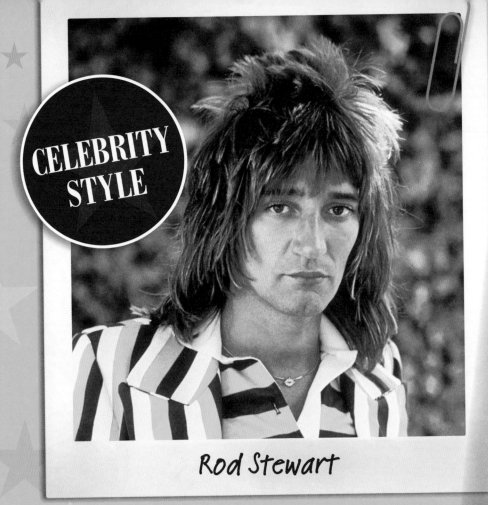

Rod Stewart

Who could resist the tousled, beach-blond locks of this aging rock-dog with a bad boy attitude? Don't be deceived by the bed-head look, this display of canine carelessness is actually meticulously maintained. Keeping it short and spiky at the back, he lets a couple of love locks drift into those big brown eyes. He Wears it so Well, what woman could resist? OK, so he might be a little bit older in dog years, but this pooch is still one headline-grabbing hound whose hair keeps him Forever Young. Just don't let him overdo it chasing Moggie May.

Dog Hair
DISASTERS

Accessories are great, but less is really more.

Not every dog can be an Einstein, and some experiments backfire.

Never leave a job half done.

After a long night out, it'll take more than a side pony to refresh those lank locks.

KODOG

KODOG

Remember to give your hair a final brush before you leave the house.

A mohawk on your head, legs and chest? I hope you know what you're doing, kid.

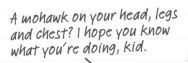

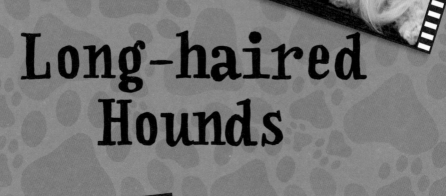

Long-haired Hounds

Cher

Not just a dog for Gypsies, Tramps and Thieves, this pretty pooch knows that she's Got You, Babe. Long, flowing black locks and a butterfly on her butt make this bitch of Eastwick look a real feisty canine character whose bark is as bad as her bite, and this puppy sure knows how to attract attention. Keep her on a healthy diet to ensure those tresses stay as strong as she is.

Comme les chiens

Le Chic Chien

You can't teach an old dog new tricks... but sometimes you don't need to. If your dog is more of a carefully coiffed cougar than a young whippet, then forget all the bells and whistles, curlers and cuts! Sometimes all you need is the perfectly placed accessory to offset her classic Parisian chic à la chienne. A dusky pink corsage lends a girlish glow to the greying lady hound and adds a classic 50s look. With a varied diet and plenty of exercise, a greying dog's coat can look particularly distinguished and glossy. Of course, if she's a pooch who likes to preen, brushing each side a hundred times a day can't hurt either.

ACCESSORIES: Beads

For aging hippy hounds, beach-bum breeds and laid-back Lassies, the beaded braid is the ultimate in low-maintenance, high-impact hair styling. A nod to traditional African cornrows, this style is a splash of summer colour for even the drabbest dog. Plaits should be tight, but start an inch or so down the shaft to avoid pulling too tightly on the fur, threading in beads as you go. A word of warning: while, with the proper care, humans can leave these in for weeks, an active dog will soon make a matted mess of these braids.

Jennifer Aniston

The 'Rachel' might have been a hair flop best left in the 90s (and definitely a difficult one for a dog to pull off), but Jennifer Aniston's still got plenty to offer the world of hairstyles – including doggie dos. With her lustrous locks, this pup has got that look of wholesome beauty and easy glamour that's sure to turn heads. Preen your pooch like this before taking her to the park, and she's sure to make a few Friends. Just be careful you don't run into a Brad Pitbull.

The Drama Queen

If your dog has animal magnetism, an auteur's hauteur and a taste for the dramatic, you need a hairstyle worthy of her trailblazing iconic status. A big personality equals big hair and a superstar equals a super-quiff. Back comb for your life and don't be afraid to go for width as well as height – this spotlight-loving pooch will take all the attention she can get... and then some. A word of caution: no diva would ever leave the house looking less than perfect, so make sure her silhouette is all clean lines and striking shapes before you take her out for her close-up.

Unleash the dark side of your dog with the long, Byronesque locks of the grizzly goth. With a widow's peak, a flowing fur cape and dark eyes on a deathly white face, this pale puppy is a true creature of the night. He'll only sleep in a velvet-lined canine-crypt and is most often found skulking in the shadows or yowling about his feelings to The Cure. Let him show off his Dark Lord look on a midnight walk through a nearby graveyard and watch him howl his angst at the moon.

The Goth

CELEBRITY STYLE

Britney

🐾 No dog is totally cute and cuddly, as anyone who has to pick up their Oopsies!... I Did it Again will know. You've got to accept that your precious little pop-pup sometimes likes to be a bit of a bad girl. For the puppy-turned-bitch who's not that innocent, sometimes a makeover is what it takes to show the world they've grown up. A set of downright dirty dreads will give a bit of edge to this once clean-cut canine. They can be easily achieved with natural products, but shouldn't be left in too long or they'll get lank and grubby.

78

One dog! One life! Let's get together, and feel alright.

The Dreadlock

Hairy hounds with a laid-back attitude can't fail with a set of doggy dreadlocks to keep them out of trouble. Unlike hippies at festivals, who just can't be bothered washing, these dreads keep your pooch in pristine condition and mean that when you take him for a walk, he doesn't bring half the park home with him. More Dog Marley than Snoop Dogg, this is man's best friend at his friendliest - a walking cloud of shaggy pelt with a smile at the end.

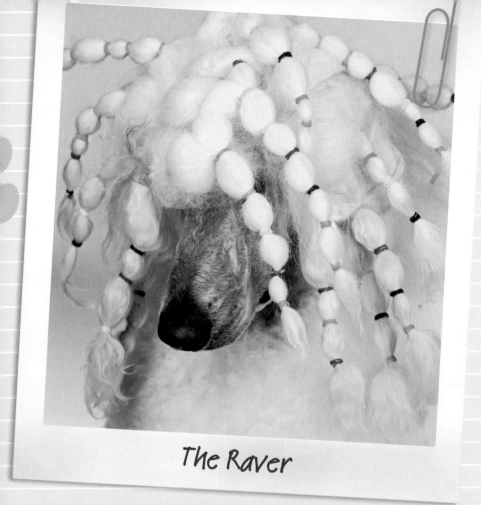

The Raver

This real nocturnal animal goes wild for downright dirty dance steps and the only stick she'll fetch is a glowstick. If this sounds like your dog, you've got yourself a club-crazy canine. To give this hell-raising hound hair she'll go raving mad for, separate the hair into sections, twist slightly to keep together, and then use thin hair elastics into the shaft at short intervals to create an easy dreadlocked effect. Multicoloured or neon hair ties are mandatory, but glow-in-the-dark ones are even better – they make it easier to spot her sneaking out to all-night raves.

THE BODY ISSUE:
All-over Glamour

Who said trains were for wedding dresses?

Not to be snubbed, a fuller coat around the chest can give a stately air.

Whoever said blondes had more fun had never met a redhead. This long, long-haired pup can boast a whole foot of fur coat and a stunning silhouette.

KODOG

KODOG

Just like a blushing bride with her dress spread out beneath her, your puppy's long locks make a dramatic snap.

Monochrome is a classic look that's easy to pull off.

KODOG

KODOG

KODOG

KODOG

KODOG

These doggy locks are perfectly kept, but it's hard to tell which end's the front and which is the back.

CELEBRITY STYLE

The Olsen Twins

With their long, blonde locks and signature sartorial style, these almost identical pop pooches look older than their dog years. Used to being lavished with attention from an early age, the Howlsen Twins are always impeccably well groomed and can't help chasing the spotlight. Dogged followers of fashion, they have strong views about the kind of canine carriers and leashes they'll be seen out in, although they did court controversy by stepping out in fur that wasn't their own.

The Farrah Flick

The face that launched a thousand flicks, Farrah Fawcett's long, blonde, bouncy curls look just as gorgeous on a long-haired dog and are perfect for any glamorous hound with a nose for trouble. Best achieved with a barrel brush or large roller, the flick is easy to style but might need a bit of product to hold it in place as she bounds off in search of criminals to catch or leaps downstairs to listen to the answering machine.

The Pocahontas

For a dog who loves getting back to nature, what could be better than these Pocahontas-style pigtails? Best on long-haired dogs, just three hair ties on the hair hanging down from each ear transforms a shaggy mane into a simple, serene style. Just be careful to tie only around the hair, not the ear itself. For added effect, pull back the hair from the front of the face in a topknot to let her catch a glimpse of her spirit human while she's out and about.

Amy Winehouse

You try to make her tame her beehive, but she says 'No, no, no'. If your soulful diva dog has unruly hair as big as her voice, make the most of it, and back comb it into a stylish 60s beehive that will really turn heads. For extra height and volume, follow Amy's own example and use a hairpiece (either human or made from a collection of your dog's own hair – though you might want to give it a shampoo first). This diva is a wild child at heart, so make sure you keep her on a tight leash on your nights out.

The Beehive

The style of choice for showy Shih Tzus in the know, the beehive makes a mean impression that's somewhere between a topknot and a turban. The trick to this is that it's a two-tier system – first separate a small strand at the front of the forehead, back comb and fix, then pull out a larger section behind that and do the same, fixing the show bow between the two. The result? A furry fan spread out across the head, making your diminutive dog that little bit more statuesque. A stern expression and severe whiskers add to the gravitas.

Is your dog the king of cool and the leader of the pack in the park? For a hound who howls like Bowie and swaggers like Jagger, nothing short of a full hair-metal hairstyle would do him justice. Like all the greatest rockers of the 70s and 80s, he's already furnished with the fullest fur coat money can buy. All that remains if he and his Muttley Crue want to rock this look all night long is to tease his long hair out, back comb it to within an inch of its life and set with sugar and water.

The Rock Legend

Beyoncé

This Sasha Fierce-some hound needs a ferocious hairstyle and there's no messing with this Amazonian afro. Smart, sassy and resplendent, the teased-out terrier-curls can be shaped into a Pooch-i-licious hairstyle your pup will love. Use hair elastics to make loose bunches if you want to retain some shape, and set with non-toxic hairspray if necessary. If you like it, then you should put a leash on it – and show it off to the world.

Dog Hair DISASTERS!

Hair extensions shouldn't look like a tired tarantula resting on his head.

Sometimes styling aids are fighting a losing battle.

When adding a splash of colour to a coat, make sure it's just a splash...

KODOG

KODOG

KODOG

Wigs can be a great way to vamp up a look, but try to choose one that's shorter than the dog wearing it.

Wind machines should be used in moderation.

Dazzling diamonds are all very well, but a lady wants to sort out her moustache before she steps out.

Acknowledgements

Age Fotostock Pixmann 14; View Stock 71. **Alamy** Dara Kushner 67 al; Fancy 44; Farlap 86; Pictorial Press 74; Pilchards 34 l; Pixmann 58; Stanislav Toloubaev 59; World Travel Collection 33. **Animal Photography** Alice van Kempen 62; Alex Grace 66 l; Eva-Maria Kramer 35 ar; Julie Poole 83 al. **Ardea** Jean Michel-Labat 51, 67 bl, 82 r; John Daniels 61 br. **Corbis** Bettmann 42; DLILLC 43; Edward Le Poulin 84; Joe Giron 50; LaCoppola & Meier 81; Mitchell Gerber 70; Moodboard 91; Nir Elias 95 bl; Push Pictures 15; Reuters 78; Richard Olivier 46; Tae Photography/First Light 63; Yann Arthus-Bertrand 95 ar. **Dorling Kindersley** Dave King 82 l; Tracy Morgan 65, 93. **FLPA** Bernd Brinkmann/Imagebroker 87; Chris Brignell 11. **Fotolia** CallallooCandcy 41; CallallooAlexis 79; Eric Isselée 35 bl, 67 br, 83 ar & br, 95 al; iNNOCENt 30; posh 90; TierfotografieWinter 95 br; Vitalij Geraskin 40. **Getty Images** age fotostock/Henryk T Kaiser 24; Anthony Harvey/WireImage 88; Christian Alminana/WireImage 26; Frank Edwards/Fotos International 12; Jade Brookbank 52; Jason Merritt 32; Jean-Paul Aussenard 92; Laurie Rubin 27; Meredith Parmelee 61 bl; Michael Ochs Archives 54; QuimGranell 57; Redferns 64; Russell K Scheid 61 ar; Tim Flach 10; Tracy Morgan/Dorling Kindersley 61 al. **Image Source** Rachael McKenna 72. **Kimball Stock** Labat-Rouquette 29; Mark McQueen 34 r; Nick Ridley 48; Winter-Churchill 76, 89. **The Kobal Collection** MGM 18. **Nature Picture Library** Adriano Bacchella 39, 55. **Press Association Images** Landov 25. **Rex Features** Giraffe News 73; Nils Jorgensen 60 r; Roger Bamber 38; Solent News 66 r. **SuperStock** Juniors 85; Nature PL 47, 75. **Thinkstock** BananaStock 67 ar; David de Lossy/Photodisc 53; Hemera 19, 21; iStockphoto 13, 16, 17, 20, 22-23, 28, 31, 35 al & br, 45, 49, 56, 60 l, 77, 80, 83 bl, 94 l & r

Commissioning Editor: Sarah Ford
Managing Editor: Clare Churly
Designer: Eoghan O'Brien
Layout Design: Clare Barber
Cover Design: Hugh Schermuly
Picture Research: Roland and Sarah Smithies
Senior Production Controller: Caroline Alberti